W9-BAH-066

BUILT FOR SPEED

CONCORDE

Suzanne J. Murdico

HIGH
interest
books

Children's Press
A Division of Grolier Publishing
New York / London / Hong Kong / Sydney
Danbury, Connecticut

Book Design: MaryJane Wojciechowski and Michael DeLisio
Contributing Editor: Jeri Cipriano

Photo Credits: Cover © Richard Hamilton Smith/Corbis; pp. 4 © AFP/Corbis;
pp. 6, 17, 22 © Reuters NewMedia Inc./Corbis; pp. 9, 15 ©Bettmann/Corbis;
pp. 11 © Marc Garanger/Corbis; pp. 12, 30 © Jim Sugar Photography/Corbis;
pp. 21 © Joel W. Rogers/Corbis; pp. 24, 36, 38 © Dean Congers/Corbis; pp. 28
© Mike Reed; Eye Ubiquitous/Corbis; pp. 33 © L. Clarke/Corbis; pp. 35
© Indexstock

Visit Children's Press on the Internet at:
http://publishing.grolier.com

Library of Congress Cataloging-in-Publication Data

Murdico, Suzanne J.
    Concorde / by Suzanne J. Murdico.
    p. cm. —(Built for speed)
    Includes bibliographical references and index.
    ISBN 0-516-23158-8 (lib. bdg.) —ISBN 0-516-23261-4 (pbk.)
    1. Concorde (Jet transports)—Juvenile literature. [1. Concorde (Jet
transports) 2. Jet planes.] I. Title. II. Built for speed.
    TL685.7 .M847 2000
    629.133'349—dc21
                                                                063896

CONTENTS

INTRODUCTION

Here's a riddle: Karen Jenkins lives in London, England. She needs to travel to New York City for a business trip. The distance is nearly 3,500 miles (5,635 km). On Monday morning, Karen takes a 9:00 A.M. flight out of London. She arrives in New York at 7:40 A.M. the same morning. That's nearly 1 ½ hours earlier than her London flight! How is this possible?

The answer is: Karen flew on the Concorde. The Concorde is a supersonic transport, or SST. Supersonic means traveling faster than the speed of sound. Standard jets are called *subsonic* because they travel at speeds less than the speed of sound.

This Concorde is coming in for a landing at an international airport.

The flight from London to New York takes nearly 8 hours on a regular, or subsonic, jet. On the Concorde, however, the same flight takes only 3 hours and 40 minutes. In addition, there is a five-hour time difference between London and New York. The Concorde's amazing speed, plus the time difference, allows Concorde passengers to arrive in New York almost 1 ½ hours *earlier* than when they left London.

The Concorde is a modern wonder of technology. It was developed in the 1970s as a way to transport travelers quickly between Europe and the United States. Today, it remains the only passenger transport that travels faster than the speed of sound.

A Concorde takes flight.

DEVELOPMENT OF THE CONCORDE

In 1956, engineers from Great Britain and France began developing a passenger plane that could fly faster than the speed of sound. At first, they worked separately. But as time went on, they realized that it made more sense to work together. In 1962, the British and French governments agreed to combine their efforts to develop the first supersonic transport—the Concorde.

In 1969, the Concorde made its first flight, taking off from Toulouse, France. Just one year later, the Concorde made its first flight at supersonic speed. And in 1976, the first passengers flew on the new SST. Today, there are

The Wright brothers were flying planes such as this one as early as 1911.

twelve Concorde SSTs in service—seven with British Airways and five with Air France.

The Concorde takes off on its first flight from Toulouse, France, in 1969.

This Concorde meter is registering a speed of Mach 2.

HOW FAST IS A CONCORDE JET?

Concorde jets are the fastest passenger jets in service today. Subsonic jets, such as Boeing 747s, fly at about 600 miles (966 km) per hour. The Concorde, however, travels at Mach 2.

Mach is a unit of measurement named after Ernst Mach, an Austrian physicist. Mach 1 equals the speed of sound, or 675 miles (1,087 km) per hour. Mach 2 is twice the speed of sound. That means that the Concorde cruises at an incredible 1,350 miles (2,173 km) per hour!

Even at takeoff, the Concorde is faster than any other commercial plane in the sky. It can accelerate from 0 to 225 miles (362 km) per hour in only 30 seconds! And, while subsonic planes lift off at 185 miles (298 km) per hour, the Concorde is capable of lifting off at an amazing 250 miles (402.5 km) per hour.

Breaking the Sound Barrier

Each time a Concorde jet reaches Mach 1, it breaks the sound barrier. And each time the sound barrier is broken, a sonic boom is produced. This sound is so loud that it can rattle or even break windows on the ground below. The sonic boom is created because a Concorde flies faster than the air moves around it. Rather than slicing through the air, the plane pushes the air. This action forms a cone-shaped shock wave, which creates the loud boom we hear.

CONCORDE VERSUS SUBSONIC JETS

The chart below compares features of the Concorde with those of a Boeing 747 — a standard subsonic jet.

	Concorde SST	Boeing 747
Cruising speed	1,350 miles (2,173 kilometers) per hour	600 miles (966 kilometers) per hour
Cruising altitude	60,000 feet (18,288 meters)	35,000 feet (10,688 meters) 40,000 feet (12,192 meters)
Flight time — London to New York	3 hours and 40 minutes	About 8 hours
Number of passengers	100	416

A Concorde flies at an altitude of sixty thousand feet.

HOW HIGH DOES THE CONCORDE FLY?

The Concorde cruises at an altitude as high as 60,000 feet (18,288 m). That's higher than any other passenger plane. Passengers on the Concorde fly above 90 percent of Earth's atmosphere. At that altitude, the sky is a deep bluish purple. And there is no rain, sleet, or snow because the Concorde flies above the weather. For this reason, Concorde passengers are not bothered by the bumps or turbulence often felt on subsonic planes. A flight on the Concorde is smooth sailing!

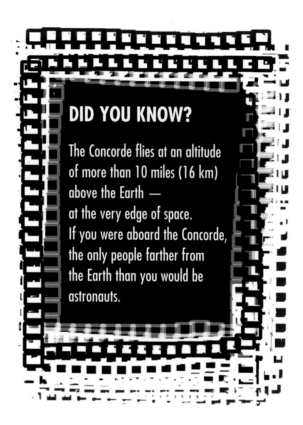

DID YOU KNOW?

The Concorde flies at an altitude of more than 10 miles (16 km) above the Earth — at the very edge of space. If you were aboard the Concorde, the only people farther from the Earth than you would be astronauts.

The Concorde's narrow body helps it reach supersonic speeds.

How can the Concorde fly at more than twice the speed, or velocity, of a subsonic jet? The answer lies in the aircraft's aerodynamic design. The Concorde has a slender, dartlike body, long nose, and short, narrow wing. These features create an attractive appearance and make the Concorde easy to spot in a crowd of standard planes. But the Concorde wasn't built for good looks. It was built for speed.

Brian Calvert, a Concorde pilot, said of the aircraft's sleek design: "Concorde's visual appeal exists quite separately from its function. Yet function dictated every line, every twist in the wing, the stalky nose leg, the pointed, drooping nose."

BODY

The Concorde's body is much narrower than that of subsonic jets. This shape helps the Concorde reach supersonic speeds. It allows the plane to slice through the air with less wind resistance than standard jets have.

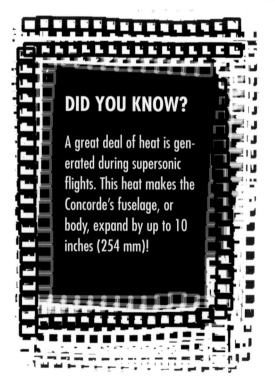

DID YOU KNOW?

A great deal of heat is generated during supersonic flights. This heat makes the Concorde's fuselage, or body, expand by up to 10 inches (254 mm)!

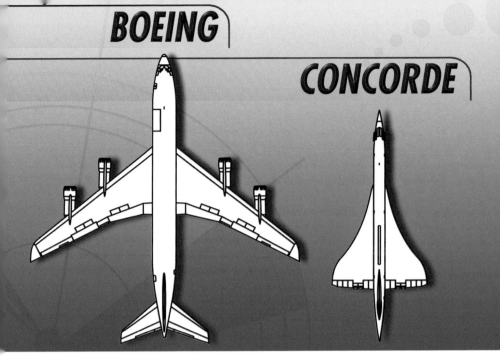

There is a great difference between the wings of a Boeing and the wings of the Concorde.

Another important factor in the Concorde's body design is its lightweight construction. It is easier for a lighter plane to travel at high speeds. So the Concorde is built mainly of an aluminum alloy, which is lighter than many other construction materials.

But there is a downside to the Concorde's narrow body shape and light weight. The number of passenger seats is very limited. Most subsonic jets carry several hundred passengers. But the Concorde carries only one hundred people. The Concorde has just one center aisle and twenty-five rows of seats. There are four passengers per row—two on either side of the aisle.

WING

One of the Concorde's most important design features is the wing. After researching many wing designs, the Concorde's engineers chose the delta. The delta wing is well suited for Mach 2 travel because it's specially designed to reduce drag, or friction, at high speeds. The Concorde's delta wing was modeled after the Fairey Delta 2, a military jet.

NOSE

One of the first things that many people notice about the Concorde is its unusual nose. It's much longer and more pointy than that of other aircraft. This needle-shaped nose helps the Concorde to pierce through the air with the least amount of resistance.

This view of the Concorde shows its very unusual nose.

During landing, though, the long nose is a disadvantage. The Concorde doesn't have the standard flaps or slats that most planes have to help them land. So the Concorde requires a more upward angle to land than do subsonic planes. But its long nose makes it difficult for the pilots to see the runway clearly. Concorde engineers found a unique solution to this problem: They made the Concorde's nose adjustable. During landing, the pilots can lower the nose by 12.5 degrees for clear visibility.

The Concorde's nose can get very hot during flight. It can heat up to 261° F (127° C). That's hotter than boiling water! To protect the flight-deck windows from this heat, a glass visor is built into the nose cone. The visor is made of several layers of special glass that can withstand these high temperatures.

This is an early 1968 prototype of today's Concorde.

Behind the SCENES

It took many highly-trained professionals to build the Concorde. Designers and engineers spent many long hours developing the Concorde. They faced many challenges because it was the first supersonic transport.

It also takes a lot of training to fly a Concorde. Once the Concorde was ready, pilots and other flight crew members had to learn special procedures. They tested the SST to make sure it was safe for passengers. Today, the Concorde flies thousands of passengers a year to their destinations. Each trip takes about half the time it would take on a standard jet!

Engineers had to create special brakes for the Concorde when it lands. This picture shows a Concorde that has just landed.

DESIGNERS AND ENGINEERS

The Concorde's designers and engineers had to be very creative. An SST had never been built. They had to find solutions to design problems that didn't exist on other planes. These creative solutions led to the development of several important technical achievements.

Technical Firsts

The Concorde lands at a very high speed. Engineers had to find a way to keep the brakes from locking during a landing. They designed a special electronic antiskid system. This anti-lock braking system, originally designed for the Concorde, is now used in many cars.

Another technical first was a set of special electronic controls. These controls, known as a fly-by-wire system, soon were being used on many other aircraft. The Concorde's engineers also were pioneers in new technology such as welding with lasers and using computers to

Milestones in

AVIATION

1903 Near Kitty Hawk, North Carolina, Wilbur and Orville Wright make the first powered plane flight with a person aboard.

The first scheduled passenger airline service transports people between St. Petersburg, Florida, and Tampa, Florida. **1914**

1927 Charles Lindbergh completes the first solo nonstop transatlantic flight.

Flying a Bell X-1 plane, American pilot Chuck Yeager becomes the first person to fly faster than the speed of sound. **1947**

1953 Jacqueline Cochran becomes the first woman to break the sound barrier.

Mach 2 – twice the speed of sound – is reached for the first time. The plane is a Tupolev Tu-144. **1968**

1976 Concorde begins its first scheduled supersonic passenger service.

guide machinery. Although these techniques are commonly used today, the Concorde's engineers were ahead of their time!

FLIGHT CREW

The Concorde is not just an ordinary plane. Not just any pilot can fly it. Concorde pilots must complete regular pilot training plus six months of intensive Concorde training. According to British Airways: "Only fifty pilots and flight engineers are qualified to fly British Airways Concorde. In total, there have been more NASA astronauts than Concorde pilots."

Each time a Concorde jet leaves the ground, nine flight crew members are aboard. A pilot, copilot, and flight engineer operate the plane from the cockpit. They have a combined total of fifty years of flying experience. In addition, six flight attendants assist the pilots and take care of the passengers.

Three Concorde pilots, with more than fifty years of experience between them, work in the cockpit.

Flying on CONCORDE

Picture this: You're on a 10:00 A.M. flight from Paris, France, to New York City. You're sitting next to the window in a soft, gray leather seat. The person next to you is enjoying the morning paper. Two other travelers are seated in your row on the other side of the aisle. There are a total of one hundred passengers aboard the aircraft. Each has paid $10,000 for a ticket.

A flight attendant walks down the aisle, handing out menus. You choose your main course from a variety of tempting selections. Your lunch is a four-course meal. The food tastes good enough to be served at a gourmet restaurant!

The captain announces that you're cruising at an altitude of 60,000 feet (18,288 m). You look out your window. You see the Earth below

Passengers are served fancy meals on the Concorde.

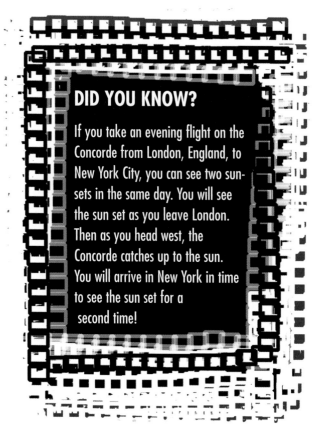

DID YOU KNOW?

If you take an evening flight on the Concorde from London, England, to New York City, you can see two sunsets in the same day. You will see the sun set as you leave London. Then as you head west, the Concorde catches up to the sun. You will arrive in New York in time to see the sun set for a second time!

as if you were viewing it from space. The window feels warm even though the outside air temperature at that altitude is extremely cold. The plane is traveling so fast, it creates a friction that heats up the air temperature.

The Concorde flies so high, it gets above the weather.

Before you know it, the captain announces arrival in New York. It seems as if you've traveled only a short distance. In fact, the flight was so fast, there wasn't even time for a movie!

The aircraft taxis to a stop. You adjust your watch to U.S. time. You see that it's only 8:45 A.M. You've actually gained time and you've traveled more than 3,600 miles (5,796 km). You've just experienced a flight on the Concorde!

CONCORDE DESTINATIONS

Concorde passengers can select from a variety of departure and destination cities. In the United States, New York City is the most common choice. In Europe, London and Paris are the usual departure and destination cities.

Most Concorde flights are transatlantic. That means that they cross the Atlantic Ocean. They do this to keep the noise of the sonic boom from bothering people on the ground. The Concorde doesn't break the sound barrier and reach its supersonic speed until it's over the ocean.

Concorde pilots get important information from air traffic controllers on the ground.

THE CONCORDE'S FUTURE

For more than thirty years, the Concorde had one of the best safety records in aviation. But in the summer of 2000, a terrible tragedy tarnished this nearly perfect record. An Air France Concorde crashed just minutes after takeoff. One of the engines had caught on fire, and the pilot lost control of the plane. The Concorde crashed into a hotel near Paris, France. All one hundred passengers and nine crew members were killed. Five people on the ground also died.

As a result of the accident, the twelve Concorde planes still in use were temporarily retired for a period of time for improvements to be made that would ensure the safety of the aircrafts when they go back into service.

The Next Concorde?

Several countries have spent a great deal of time and money trying to develop the next generation of Concorde jet.

It takes a large team of experts and workers to construct a Concorde.

Here, a technician works on the Concorde's cockpit.

A European project had been planned for a fleet of Super Concordes. These planes would be an improved version of the Concorde. They would be designed to carry two hundred passengers instead of only one hundred. And the Super Concorde would travel farther than the Concorde. In the United States, NASA spent ten years planning a supersonic transport program. But the SST projects in Europe and the United States both were dropped. The engineers could not develop a cost-effective design.

Design Challenges

Before a new and improved Concorde can be developed, engineers must find ways to overcome several design challenges. These include:

- **Noise** The Concorde is very noisy both during takeoff and when supersonic speed is reached. Some cities won't even allow the Concorde to take off from their airports because of the noise. The Concorde's noise levels would have to be reduced before it could fly over populated areas.

- **Ozone** To save on fuel, a new Concorde would fly at a higher altitude. This altitude would be closer to the ozone layer. But the aircraft's exhaust could destroy some of the ozone. That would create an environmental problem. To avoid this, engineers would need to find a way to reduce the amount of exhaust produced by the new plane.

- **Weight** Future Concordes would probably travel at *hypersonic* speeds, such as Mach 3. It also would travel greater distances than the current Concorde.

To do so, the new aircraft's frame would need to be 30 percent lighter than the original Concorde.

- **Expense** The Concorde is very expensive to operate. One reason is the plane's small size. It can carry only a small number of passengers. Despite the price of ten thousand dollars a single ticket, there aren't enough passenger fares to cover expenses. The aircraft requires a huge amount of fuel to achieve supersonic speed. A new Concorde would have to be more economical to operate.

First, engineers would have to find solutions to these problems. Then improved supersonic planes could be developed. For now, though, new developments are uncertain. Regardless of the future, one fact remains true. The Concorde was the first supersonic transport and has remained a one-of-a-kind marvel for more than thirty years.

Fact Sheet

ENGINE: Rolls Royce/SNECMA Olympus 593
    with afterburners

LENGTH OF FUSELAGE: 231 feet (70.5 meters)

WEIGHT: 410,000 pounds (184,500 kg)

CRUISING SPEED: Mach 2

SPEED RECORD: New York City to London, England, in
    2 hours, 52 minutes, and 59 seconds

CRUISING ALTITUDE: 60,000 feet (18,288 meters)

NUMBER OF PASSENGERS: 100

TEMPERATURE IN FLIGHT: up to 261° F (127° C)
    at the nose

NEW YORK-LONDON TICKET PRICE: approximately
    $10,000 round-trip

NEW WORDS

aerodynamic designed to reduce drag and improve fuel efficiency

altitude the height of an object above land

atmosphere the air surrounding Earth

drag the force of the air that pulls against a plane's forward motion

fuselage the central body of an aircraft, which holds the passengers, crew, and cargo

hypersonic more than three times the speed of sound

Mach a unit for measuring the speed of sound; Mach 1 equals the speed of sound

ozone the layer of atmosphere that protects the Earth from the sun's ultraviolet rays

NEW WORDS

sonic boom a loud sound made when a shock wave is formed as an airplane reaches the speed of sound

sound barrier a sudden large increase in drag that happens when an airplane approaches the speed of sound

subsonic below the speed of sound

supersonic transport a vehicle that travels faster than the speed of sound

turbulence irregular motion in the atmosphere that causes a bumpy plane flight

velocity speed

wind resistance the pressure of the air against the plane

For Further READING

Aaseng, Nathan. *Breaking the Sound Barrier.*
New York: Julian Messner, 1991.

Chant, Christopher. *Specialized Aircraft.*
Broomall, PA: Chelsea House Publishers, 1999.

Graham, Ian. *Aircraft.* Chatham, NJ: Raintree
Steck-Vaughn, 1998.

Taylor, Richard L. *The First Supersonic Flight:
Captain Charles E. Yeager Breaks the Sound
Barrier First Books.* New York: Franklin Watts,
Inc., 1997.

RESOURCES

Organizations

Federal Aviation Administration (FAA)
800 Independence Avenue
Washington, DC 20591
www.faa.gov

National Aeronautics and Space Administration (NASA)
Washington, DC 20546-0001
www.nasa.gov

Web Sites

Aerospace Team Online
http://quest.arc.nasa.gov/aero/index.html
The men and women of the Aerospace Team will answer your questions and teach you more about how planes fly. You can read actual field journals from the team and look at the photo gallery.

RESOURCES

The K-8 Aeronautics Internet Textbook
http://wings.ucdavis.edu/
This site allows you to choose a reading level and learn the principles of flight. It includes information about the history of flight, an image gallery, and lots of fun facts.

NASA Langley Research Center's Kids Corner
http://kidscorner.larc.nasa.gov/
Take a guided tour through this Web site and learn to design and build your own virtual aircraft. This site includes a chat room and a career corner.

INDEX

A
aerodynamic, 17
altitude, 15, 31
anti-lock braking
   system, 26
atmosphere, 15
aviation, 37

B
body, 18, 19

D
drag, 20

E
engineer, 10, 20, 23,
   25, 26, 38, 39, 40
expense, 40

F
flight crew, 29
fly-by-wire system, 26
fuselage, 18

H
hypersonic, 39

M
Mach, 12, 13

N
nose, 17, 18, 21, 23

O
ozone, 39

INDEX

About the Author

Suzanne J. Murdico is a freelance writer who has authored numerous books for children and teens.